FINDING O

WRITE OUT LOUD WOKING

THE FIRST SIX YEARS
2016-2022

THE WOODENER PRESS

ISBN: 9798351891125
Published by The Woodener Press
Copyright remains with the individual poets.
All rights reserved.

https://www.facebook.com/search/top?q=write+out+loud+woking

Please direct any enquires about Write Out Loud (Woking) live sessions
to Rodney Wood at rodneytwood@gmail.com and to Write Out Loud
(Woking) Zoom to Greg Freeman at gfreem@ntlworld.com

Acknowledgements: I would like to thank the editors or publishers who
first printed these poems:

David Andrew ('Grandfather') in *Ventriloquist's Dummy* (Lapwing, 2015);
Aileen Ballantyne (' Lockerbie: Pan Am, Flight 103 - The Investigator')
in *Taking Flight* (Luath Press, 2019);
Denise Bundred ('Les Tournesols') in *The Dark Horse;*
Kitty Coles ('The Seal Wife') in *Seal Wife* (Indigo Dreams 2017);
Greg Freeman ('Backroom Boys'), in *Trainspotters* (Indigo Dreams,
2015);
Pete Jardine ('Secret Bath Spaniel'), Poem Of The Day for *Richmond
Arts*;
Christopher Johnson ('Came Back') in *Sublime*;
Alex Josephy ('For a Journey to the Forest in Time of Snow') in *Ink
Sweat and Tears*;
Andy B.J. Low ('Birth Of A Poet') in *The Pop Up Anthology of the
1000 Monkeys* (Dempsey and Windle, 2014);
Alwyn Marriage ('Speculate') in *Possibly a Pomegranate: Celebrating
Womankind (*Palewell Press, 2022);
Tom McColl ('The Chalk Fairy') in *Being With Me Will Help You Learn*
(Listen Softly London Press, 2016);
Patrick Osada ('Refugees') in *How The Light Gets In* (Dempsey and
Windle, 2018);
Brit Schneuer ('The Reservation') in *The Cat Comes and with her the
Garden (*2022*);*
Rodney Wood ('The Night I Told Genesis to Fuck Off') in
spillingcocoa.com.

Printed and bound in the UK

Table of Contents

Introduction: Write Out Loud Woking – the first six years

Welcome to this anthology of poetry from Write Out Loud Woking, an open-mic poetry group that has been meeting in the Woking area and online for half a dozen years. We've called this anthology Finding our Voices, to try and encapsulate the founding principles we believe in about open-mic poetry – that it should be open to all, that it can help people express themselves, develop self-confidence, exorcise demons, share stories. This collection of poems gives a flavour of the rich diversity of voices that we have heard over the years.

Our open-mic group began at the New Inn in Send, a pub on the banks of the Wey Navigation, in a village just outside Woking, back in May 2016. Rodney Wood, who lives in Farnborough, had been saying to fellow poet Greg Freeman for some time that they ought to start an open-mic poetry night in Woking. And Greg agreed. A town the size of Woking - the home of The Jam - required one. The question was, where?

The New Inn solved that problem, for the next two years at least. We had the use of its dining area at the back of the pub on Monday nights, once a month. Our name appeared on its blackboard of events. We took a picture for a launch and sent it in to the local paper, which published it. Poetry friends came to support us. Sometimes it was a bit of a squash, sometimes not so much. After the first night Greg got hold of a mic and amp that helped us to hear some of our quieter poets. From the outset Rodney and Greg shared compering duties. Write Out Loud Woking – in line with the ethos of our international website Write Out Loud - was always intended to provide a place for any poet who wanted to come and read for five minutes. We did introduce guest poets after a while, with longer reading slots, but only on an occasional basis. That open-to-all ethos continued when we moved to the café of the Lightbox museum and art gallery in Woking. We were very grateful to the New Inn for hosting us for two years, but this was a more convenient venue. Write Out Loud Woking was now actually in Woking at last, and funnily enough, on the banks of another canal, this time the Basingstoke. With public transport access and improved car parking, and publicity on the Lightbox's own website, our numbers grew. Often we had no idea who was going to walk in through the door and ask to read. That was the beauty of it.

We also took part in three Lightbox literary festivals, providing between three and five hours of open-mic poetry on a Saturday in the Lightbox cafe, and with guest poets that included Elvis McGonagall, Susan Evans, Robert Garnham, Geoff Allnutt, Annum Salman, Maggie

Sawkins, Alison Hill, and Racker Donnelly, a former local Labour councillor turned performance poet, whose epic poem about the history of Woking lingers long in the memory.

Then came lockdown, and the Lightbox was forced to close its doors, for what turned out to be 18 months. What to do? After a month or two, as so many other groups were doing, we turned to Zoom. And found a new lease of life. Poets joined us from all over the country, and from other countries, too. They included veteran punk poet Nick Toczek, from Bradford, who's seen and heard it all over the years. Paignton performance poet Robert Garnham, who has a special place in his heart for Woking. Disabled Wigan poet Shaun Fallows, who was thrilled to be reading online at Woking, home of his hero Paul Weller. Plus Stephen Claughton from Berkhamsted – Graham Greene's old stamping ground – who drove round the M25 to join us at the Lightbox, as well as reading with us on Zoom.

Eventually, in September 2021, we returned to the Lightbox, but kept the Zoom nights going as well. What's happened since is that some of our regulars have preferred to stay with us online, rather than return to our in-person venue. Others have opted to meet people in the flesh again, rather than gather on screen. Either choice is fine with us. It's been interesting to see how things develop, as it always has been. Certainly the reaction to our return to the Lightbox in September 2021 took us by surprise. The exhilaration of the microphone again!

Rodney has been the driving force behind this anthology, produced partly to mark the imminent departure of Greg to the north-east of England, for family reasons - although Greg still intends to instigate our monthly Zoom sessions from Northumberland. The two have quite different poetry and compering styles, and yet they've managed to rub along together successfully for the past six years. We would like to thank Mary Hely and others before her at the Lightbox for their support and help in our endeavours; and Mark, the landlord at the New Inn, who enthusiastically enabled us to kickstart this shebang.

Thanks also to our tech-savvy poet Pete Jardine, who spearheaded our eruption on to YouTube, filming our readings at the Lightbox, and then editing and processing our Zoom contributions as well. You can find them on YouTube if you type in Write Out Loud Woking.

But most of all we thanks all our poets, without which none of this could have happened - for their warmth, friendship, support, and their wonderful words.

We would like to dedicate this anthology to David Andrew, a fine poet and stalwart supporter and regular at Write Out Loud Woking until he became ill during lockdown. He died in 2022. We have also lost two other poets who read with us – Grant Tarbard, and Frances White. They won't be forgotten.

Rodney Wood and Greg Freeman
August 2022

A few comments from our poets

I would say some of my best poetry moments have been from Write Out Loud Woking (WOLW). I will never forget all the wonderful poets I met. It really opened doors for me and widened my poetry horizons.
Heather Moulson

WOLW was a lifeline during the Covid years, the warmth, wit and demotic charm of MCs Rodney and Gregg shone through despite being on a Zoom screen. There was always a good core crowd of regulars as well as newcomers, a stimulating range of voices, terrific new poems and some wonderful translations. Readings to savour and remember. Thank you.
Konstandinos Mahoney

The monthly WOLW readings run on Zoom by Greg and Rodney are one of my favourites of all such events, not least because of the caring commitment of its two stellar organisers. Their shared professionalism, compassion, and commitment gave succour, strength, and renewed faith to all of us who were lucky enough to participate. It's been an utter joy to have been one of those participants.
Nick Noczek

I have valued the company, the wonderful setting, the friendliness and the welcoming and entertaining comperes of WOLW.
Patrick Osada

WOLW is a very friendly and welcoming group. I was made to feel at home there from the start. For me, it's a safe space, in which I'm comfortable trying things out.
Stephen Claughton

The meetings have been very supportive and helped me reach new audiences for my work. Always very receptive to my audio/visual theatrics but the the actual poetry too.
Lee Campbell

I think I only came to the Lightbox sessions twice. Both times, I loved the variety of poetry performed there, and the way in which you and Greg gave a welcome to poetry from all corners of Poetry World! The warm audience response when each poet read was encouraging and heartening too. No wonder the meetings were so well attended.
Alex Josephy

Attending the zoom meetings for WOLW has brought me a great deal of happiness and I believe furthered my progress as a poet. I have always found it a supportive, intelligent, and respectful group with a good sense of fun as well. Although I haven't met most of the people in the group because of the distance involved I feel a friendship with them and look forward to seeing them all monthly. It was especially helpful through the lonely days of Covid and I'm very glad to continue to be part of this excellent group of poets.
Jacky Woods

For me, the joy of coming to WOLW was always that it was so welcoming, an ethos which you both fostered. So it was no surprise that the poets who came along were diverse and had diverse things to say, and that newcomers returned precisely because they felt welcome. To my mind, that is exactly what an open mic should be about. The guest poets were well-chosen and enjoyed their spotlight without feeling a need to be big-headed about it, which isn't always the case in my experience. The format was sensible, well-paced and encouraged poets to be both entertaining and affecting in equal measure.
Matthew Paul

I think it has been a great opportunity for the poets of the area to read and speak about their poetry regularly both live and on Zoom. This is the best thing of WOLW, the opportunity to stay connected, learning from one another and testing our poetry in the readings.
Carla Scarano

I was delighted to take part in the Zoom sessions, but a little nervous to be performing alongside real professionals. However, the welcome and support I was given by all, encouraged me to continue with my performances, and to participate in live events local to me.
Su Mitchell

David Andrew

GRANDFATHER

Walking down the backs of my life
I come upon a quiet alley
in an old town: could be here at my feet,
could be a long time ago.

Rain fallen an hour ago: is it
I walking by this fence – full assurance
of age, or some trainee man
up north forty years ago?

Grandfather, it's you waiting for me here
after all this time, expecting me
to stay straight: erect, warm, from
an age where street lights were quieter.

Your language had fewer words in it,
your life had fewer steps
because there were fewer places you
could afford to go to.

Two generations ago, an echo in rain.
How can I explain to my children
sunlight in a town dirty with mills,
the miraculous gasometers,

Territorial Halls, the gaudy stained
salvia in the municipal gardens,
and a man already old of whom
I can remember not a word.

This evening in March dark, not two
generations or forty years ago,
but up there, the end of an alley
I walk out of to where I began.

Chris Andrews

TO GREG THE GREAT

To Greg the great
Who's not afraid to stand up for what he likes or tolerates
To Greg the nicest person here
Someone I'd be happy to go for a beer

To Greg the kind
Who listens to what's on my mind
To Greg who doesn't detest rhyming pieces
Or poems I write about my nieces

Yes alliteration is cool
And as you write similes and metaphors then you're no fool
I'm here for the non-poets
Who look at your poem but do not know it

Because a non-poet expects rhyme all the time
And I'm not talking about one or two I mean line after line
Many of the poets of old did rhyme
Yet other than mainly Greg you see this as a crime

To have a book of poems that do not rhyme
Is like a song that doesn't stay in time
Sorry if my razor sharp words hurt you
But for me this feeling is true

To Greg the welcoming who makes all feel at home
Whether they be at the lightbox, on zoom or holidaying in Rome
To Greg the great I raise a glass
To the most decent person in the class.

Aileen Ballantyne

LOCKERBIE: PAN AM, FLIGHT 103 - THE INVESTIGATOR
21 December 1988

.....But I have promises to keep,
And miles to go before I sleep.....
(Robert Frost)

At Arlington Cemetery
on the longest day of darkness
the names of the dead
are intoned one by one;
an FBI man quotes Frost:
dark against light,
winter versus spring.

He lists the items he saw on the shelves
of a small wooden building in Lockerbie:
a teenager's single white sneaker,
a Syracuse college sweatshirt, never worn,
toys wrapped up for Christmas,
packed in the case of a father
who never came home.

Each charge is outlined with precision.
Robert Mueller has total recall
of all that was broken.
When the darkness falls again,
he will remember.

Trevor Breedon

SECRET AMBITION

In my first years of striving towards
your secret ambition, I could never understand
why you hated your work. Bent over books,
I dreamed of plunging through blackness
in a cage full of ragged adventurers,
helmets, knee pads and boots jostling,
snap tins hanging like spare ammo packs,
armed for the unknown, on a journey
not quite to the centre of the earth
but deep and hot enough.

I could never fathom your hours;
you were a blanketed shape on the settee
while we ate in considerate silence
and the grey morning rattle of the poker
as I lay in bed tracing the ritual: twisting
of newspaper knots, stacking of coal,
the Mirror's middle pages spread
and scorching against a standing shovel
to draw the roar of flames
up the chimney past my head.

I never saw your white smile break the grime;
'Don't bring dirt or work into the house'
was the rule. The day you returned
in shock after the roof fell, I knew
darkness and danger had tunnelled too far
to end my fascination. When you carried home
the shining black fossil imprinted
with the perfect image of a fern
I saw the reflection of its beauty in your face
and the pride in a job you could never admit.

Trisha Broomfield

CONSULATE

Smoke curls up from Consulate
inhaled and put aside,
beds are made haphazardly,
windows opened wide.
Milk forms skin on coffee cups,
clothes are washed in Tide,
cupboard's full of easy food,
Marmite and Mother's Pride.

The ironing, in date order,
grows tall upon the board;
we write our names on dusty tops,
most housework is ignored.
Meals are planned at random;
she buys the best she can afford.

Coco Pops scrunch underfoot
and grit the kitchen floor.
There always seems to be enough,
there's cash in that top drawer.
Knitting needles that once clicked
present her with a chore,
and the post delivered yesterday
still lies beside the door.

Cinzano decorates in rings
the table at her side,
nails are filed and stockings clean,
red lipstick worn with pride.
Her promises, though, often drown
as to herself she's lied,
she sucks the life from Consulate,
determined to provide.

Graham Brown

ELEPHANT IN THE ROOM

Woke up this morning with an elephant in the room
stuck in the bay window in the early hour gloom.
A grey mountain in my pied a terre – it doesn't make me smile
to see the floor wet from a jumbo jet and carpet with more pile.

Woke up this morning with an elephant in the room.
The house shook as he roared like a supersonic boom.
Then he stood up and trumpeted as loud as loud could be
in a flagrant violation of my terms of tenancy.

Woke up this morning with an elephant in the room.
Told me that his name was George and he came from Ilfracombe.
'You've gone and ruined my brand new suite. Flattened it!' I wail.
He said 'I'm sorry. Yes but DFS has got a mammoth sale!'

Woke up this morning with an elephant in the room.
How many further currant buns can a pachyderm consume?
He's eaten me out of house and home. He really cannot stay.
I've phoned the local tusk force to take the beast away.

Woke up this morning with no elephant in the room.
I strangely miss him, feel quite sad. Not the joy I would assume.
I hear a rumbling as I climb the stairs. You must be having a laugh!
There's a blinking hippopotamus wallowing in my bath.

Denise Bundred

LES TOURNESOLS

'Nothing but large Sunflowers' he writes to Émile Bernard,
'broken chrome yellows blaze on palest malachite to royal blue'.

He labours 'with the gusto of a Marseillais eating bouillabaisse'.
Four in the month — decoration for a hopeful studio.

The first — a trio in a green vase — will sell for a few hundred francs.
It has not been seen for generations.

In the second, there are three soleils (one gone to seed) and a bud.
All haloed by their complementary colours to enhance the impact.

The third contains twelve in an unstable pot — light on light
for the Yellow House. From sunrise he has to hurry as they wilt.

For the fourth he follows Manet's peonies. 'Do you remember
that one day? Pink flowers thickly impasted and not glazed.'

He imitates the varied brushstrokes but adds himself —
backlit, dazzling, inimitable.

A bouquet of fourteen and a small one added on the left. Some are
                                                                dead.
The germ of life's cycle in dried heads created directly from the tube.

In the dark days of January, he will make three copies — scattered now
to Amsterdam, Philadelphia and (he'd be proud of this) Japan.

The peonies against their white ground hang in the Musée d'Orsay.
The fifteen sunflowers are in London where children with runny noses

wriggle and grizzle while parents steam in winter coats
on a wet Sunday in November.

Lee Campbell

POSTCARDS

When the weatherman forecast hot sunny spells
In the days when trains not always ran on electric rails
British Rail carriages filled with diesel smells
I loved that trip to the coast from my hometown Tunbridge Wells

Luck always seemed to be on my side
Second class ticket, first class ride
If the ticket inspector asked I'd get teary eyed
Offer him tea out my flask and say my pet had just died
For all her airs and graces and sense of pride
Nan taught me this trick. Like me, cheeky inside
In between swimming and beach picnics
I was at work with my pencils and graphite sticks
As I was drawing on the backs of postcards, I could hear the clicks
of my Grandad on his camera taking pics
Grandad up to his latest photographic tricks
Me deciding what scene my next postcard depicts

I wish I could see in the sea
Just abstract shapes and blobs passing in front of me
Having long distance vision, it's the feel and sounds of the sea that
keeps me excited
It's the thrill of its chill that keeps me strangely delighted
I went beyond vision, embraced the seaside slapstick haptic
There's just as much pleasure in what is heard as what's seen
Sounds of the contemporary now evoking the sights of what's been
With your mates having a jolly, the joy of seaside laughter
Paired with the sad melancholy of a dog barking, looking out at sea for
his master

Quick trip, skinny dip
As I come out of the water, cover my crown jewels with a towel
if I can't see, then maybe others can't too
I guess what you choose to see is up to you

Pratibha Castle

PADRAIG – WHO DROVE THE SNAKES OUT OF IRELAND

At the allotment, daddy
forked the crumbly black earth
till the air quaked
with anticipation of excess,
me sifting stones
in search of treasure;
the robin sat, pert,
on the lip of the bucket meant
to carry spuds or cabbages,
the occasional giggle-tickle carrot
back to placate the mammy.

The bird's eye bright
with a lust for worms,
his song a crystal cataract
of merry; though none
of the seeds we sowed
ever showed head
out of the sly earth
and we saw nothing
of the slow worm
daddy promised so that,
his name being Padraig too,
I guessed he must be a saint, especially
when he himself vanished.

Though he turned up
months later
at the end of school
again and again and again
till I had to tell the mammy
where the books and toys came from
and that got me sent off
to board at St. Bridget's convent
where the head nun was nice to you
if your mammy gave her fruit cake
in a tin, bottles of orange linctus sherry,
a crocheted shawl like frothy cobwebs,
none of which my mammy could afford,
Padraig having banished more than snakes

17

Afon Claerwen

PALEO-POETOLOGY

It was all Big Pharma's fault he said
as he rattled his afternoon pills.
I suppose without this lot
I would have been gone years ago.
Yes indeed came the wise response
and all those extra poems too...

Oh no! Imagine – like global plastic
what happens to these words
when they dissolve in the ether
or go in the recycling bin and then the shredder...

Noooo...! - imagine millions of fractal haikus
floating in the atmosphere then drifting down
with the nuclear fallout and the micro-plastics
into the few remaining glaciers
in Greenland and Iceland and the Antarctic

Fractals of fractals - Rac ... tals ... fra ...
fine as gold leaf in the Anthropocene layers
of our precious planet's geological succession.

Imagine then 350 million years into the future
fine sheets of ancient slate in another time
as far forward as when we look back
at a piece of Welsh slate now, and find those tiny
one-sided micro-fern fronds - dear Graptolites

But in the future the finest Anthropocene slate
has fractals of the most exquisite words
in tiny extinct images like..
.. I love you
.. the touch of your hand
.. the fresh hay scent of your hair
.. the sapphire sky
And for a moment the future questers might forgive
the immense mountains of ancient plastic
awaiting recycling in Mother Earth's core.

Stephen Claughton

THE READING
after Catullus

The reading the other night,
Licinius, I thought it went well.
You've certainly got a gift,
a real feel for poetry,
with technical skill to die for,
a voice that's all your own
and the imagery, my God!
I'd give anything, I swear,
to come up with tropes like that.
You were turbocharged, on fire.
I, desperate to catch up,
road-tested my latest work.
It was risky, I know,
but the audience were kind –
no car crash, anyway.

Afterwards, driving home,
I couldn't settle down
for thirty motorway miles.
Speed traps hurled thunderbolts
after the unwary.
Under the gantries' limits,
we were reduced to a crawl,
like competitors keeping our lanes.
My mind, though, was still racing.
Stuck in lines of traffic,
I produced these lines of my own.
Don't laugh. You may be good,
but pride comes before a fall.
Believe me, I know.
I've seen the future, Licinius.

Kitty Coles

SEAL WIFE

The weather turns.
A wind from the north has flown in,
with its violent curse,
and it raises the waves
till I cannot shut out their yowling.

The old scars itch on my flank,
disquieted.
The hairs on my spine rise up
in the chill that presses
itself under the door,
an insinuating ghost.

The cat has wound herself
to an endless running
from one end of the house to the other,
poor bristling devil.

The grass is aching with frost.
Birds fall, small toys,
from the trees in their deaths.
The cold is murderous.

In the churchyard, the drowned
walk at noon as if it were night.
They return to old beds,
slip in by their frozen wives.

And I am numbing myself
with my baking, my stitching, by washing
the floors till the stone begins to thin.
I hide my face from the mirror:
its enquiry threatens.
If I could forget, the water could not claim me.

Michael Cutchey

AUTUMNAL CONVERSATIONS
(A Poem for Greg)

We met there,
on the hillside path
beneath a canopy of amber leaves
Together we sat
on the old bench
and talked,
Oh, how we talked
our animated faces
dappled by the sunlight,
That wry twinkle in your eyes
your sonorous voice
so filled with reflection and purpose
We felt like we could
solve all the problems in the world,
you and I, sitting on that park bench
The world turned around us,
we became its focal point
an island of stillness, picturesque
The peaceful serenity of it
still moves me, even now
remembering the joy of your company
But alas, our dappled, watercolour scene
fell at last into dusk,
time it seems, gets the best of us all
And so, we stood
buttoned up our coats
and embraced, bidding adieu to the day
Farewell my friend,
I wish you the best in all you do
and warm my heart by knowing we will meet again.

John de Prey

SHE DROPS A TEACUP

She sits alone forgetting her words.
She hasn't spoken for days.
She takes her walk to the kitchen

and back. The warmth of tea,
its ritual there to be shared.
A laughing young family passes,

the post van, a sniffing dog.
They are miles away.
Thursday's the funeral, online.

She couldn't say good bye.
A walk to the shops was life then,
when she could drive to Thursley

to see dragonflies and swallows,
when she could remark on the weather,
exchange a smile, a touch.

Will it take her too? Will she be
one of the two in "332 died today"?
Same news every day. Same assurance.

Same exasperated questions. Same excuses,
numbers and graphs, accusations.
She drops a teacup, the highlight of her day.

Alex de Suys

MEMES

I've fallen to memes, I'm not even rhyming,
The memes are so easy, it comes down to timing.
Why should I stitch up the news into verse,
When I just pinch their pictures and spin in reverse,
Or add an omission, or reveal a truth,
All so much easier with visual proof.
Yes I could tell you that this person did it,
But a pic of them doing? They will not have hid it.
And being caught out they might change or be changed,
To the next willing sock puppet in a system deranged,
Run by the Uber rich just for their whim,
Like that cretin Prince Charles let's all listen to him,
Like his great chum Klaus Schwab, who'll be owning it all,
While you will eat bugs and own nothing at all.
And I can quote you his quotes and still put things in rhyme,
But a link and a pic of him saying it's fine.
It's better than fine, it's very effective,
It's making my love of the poems defective,
So if you imagine, I'm finding it kind,
For you to bring poetry back to my mind,
For I'll tell you the truth there is less satisfaction,
In hundreds of likes and some genuine traction,
Than having a mic and a poetry crowd
And hearing you take what I'm saying out loud,
I might get a laugh, or a snort or a nod,
I may strike some people as terribly odd,
But I feel I must do this and I see you as friends,
And we must do our best for our friends in the end,
For our kids, nephews, nieces who deserve to be free,
And not simple drudges for the powers that be,
For our mums, dads and theirs to live on to old age,
And not be erased for the balance book's page,
So I've fallen to memes, I admit it it's true,
But I'd still love one day to read this out to you.

Dónall Dempsey

"M'APPARI TUTT' AMOR..."
('She appeared to me full of love...')

Here in the church
of my father's carpentry

the incense is
of pine

sunlight genuflects
through the window

wood curls
in religious ecstasy

a bluebottle
preaches an iridescent sermon

a choir of dust motes
make this a heaven

as my father hums
"M'appari tutt' amor.."

this my epiphany
of the ordinary

this the everyday
prayer

I bow my head to
the saw as it sings

"....bella si che il mio cor ..."

Janice Dempsey

ADVICE

Stirring the porridge
I think of Miss Rymer's grave.

She's passed her century if she's not in it.
I wish I'd written this,
she wrote on my homework.

Keep stirring, don't stop,
my mother always warned.

Some advice, some praise
stays with you.

Keep stirring, or life goes lumpy
and sticks.

Shaun Fallows

HOW COME?
In response to hearing 60% of deaths in the Covid pandemic were disabled.

So we don't matter
How come?
How come?
We get the bribe benefits
To just stay happy glum
So we don't matter
How come?
How come?
Cos we have the act now
Not fit for purpose
Everybody's off the hook
Feeling slightly less guilty numb
So we don't matter
How come?
How come?
Can't exercise
Can't exercise my right
No option
Is my option
How come?
How come?
Slowly I must watch you rape
My health
My life
My prospects
As casually as someone discarding chewing gum
How come?
How come?
So we don't matter
How come?
How come?
We're always the ones dealing with the consequences
In everyday mazes
While you still see disability as little more
Than experimental populous fads and fazes
So we don't matter
How come?
How come?

Cos the politicians
Seduce but still serve themselves
This silence says it all
Tory dolls in red run for a considerable sum
How come?
How come?
But its been duly noted
However long it takes
I'll hound them all the way
Cos
Disabled doesn't mean dumb

Greg Freeman

BACKROOM BOYS
i.m David Andrew

Last time in London, chanced upon this caff,
close by where I once worked. Fitted the bill;
lasagne, chips, salad, less than five quid.
"Look," you said. "Locals eat here. Must be good."
You'd arrived first. Navvies' tea on table,
exuberant, eyes gleaming: "How I love
this city!" Saw the city through your eyes,
mapped by no-nonsense, honest caffs –
HP sauce, beverages, something
bubbling behind the counter.
Steamed-up sanctuaries, hiding places
run by Italians, Cypriots, Greeks,
oases for those in the know. Only
a few yards to the bookshop, wealth
of poetry on the shelves. Pottered down
Farringdon Road, past pubs, pole-dance joints,
open mic venues; you regaling me
with exotic family histories,
cousins who lived in Kenya, Singapore.
You spied a shop that sold telescopes,
next to a place bombed in the first world war.
Battered poppies on our jackets.
Demonstrators camped outside St Paul's.
A three-piece, eastern European band
resounding under Blackfriars bridge.
"You and me, we're backroom boys" –
your parting words. This splendid autumn.
My friend, we've found our rendezvous.

Gillian Freeman

CONFESSIONS OF A SERIAL KILLER

I'm not a violent person.
Raised in a house of daily battles, dodging minefields,
I much prefer peace.
Cannot watch old war films on TV, the bloodshed and the pain too much
to bear.
But
When darkness falls, I leave the house to kill.
Armed only with the Torch of Doom and size 4 feet, I slaughter without
mercy.
Part Gertrude Jekyll, part Mr Hyde, I silently patrol the borders,
Flash the torch, swoop then stamp.
A righteous war, not for greed or hate
But protection for the helpless sitting targets.
Four sunflowers maimed and leafless, bare stalks point their
accusation:
Where were you when we needed you? Why raise us just for this?
I rampage on, trying to ignore the tiny squeals, the hopeless cringes in
the spotlight.
Later, scrubbing filth and ooze from sticky fingers
Out, out, damn slime.
Nocturnal genocide makes it hard to sleep
But miss a raid, and lie awake until the roar of tiny teeth
Jolts me up to grab my shoes and torch.
Two sole allies in the alley – a fat white toad, a tiny, frightened frog,
But where are the hedgehogs when you need them?

Andy V. Frost

WHALIGOE

I count the steps,
feel the Fish-wives lives
measured
in descent.

I see their ghosts
go empty down,
baskets full of Herring up,
thighs striding mighty,

against the elements,
bare skin blasted and hardened,
lips rouged by the salted kiss
of their fisher men.

I reach the Bink,
sit down on silent ground
amidst the Salt-house ruin
and rusty winches.

I think on the ocean,
observe the rock-perched Shag,
commune with myself
in solitude.

I'm undisturbed in this peace,
except for the clamour of gulls,
the slap of incoming waves
and the bustling ghosts.

Robert Garnham

POEM

There's a mossy rock in the forest
A place I always like to go
A mossy rock in the woods
I go there when I'm feeling low.

And I sit on the rock in the moss
And it's hard and it makes me forget
I sit on the rock in the woods
If it's damp it'll make my bum wet

There's a mossy rock in the forest
Surrounded by foliage and leaves
And big arse rhododendrons
It's a place that puts me at my ease

And I sit on the rock in the moss
And the ground it's wet and spongy
And there's mushrooms sprouting up
And other types of fungi

There's a mossy rock in the forest
Its ok I suppose it could be worse
There are badgers and squirrels in the forest
(That's it now I'm done with this verse)

And I sit on rock in the moss
I only like to sit here and ponder
And the rock is not exactly comfy
I can manage ten minute, nothing longer.

There's a mossy rock in the forest
the branches here are terribly scratchy
I try to watch some cricket on my phone
But the Wi-Fi signal here is patchy.

And I sit on the rock in the moss
And I sit on the rock in the moss
And I sit on the rock in the moss
And then my mind wanders off.

MANY A TRUE WORD ...

Never trust a poet,
they are wearing a disguise,
you might think they are listening
but they are plotting lies.
Like magpies they are spying gems
that others haven't spotted,
just watch and they will swipe them
and soon they'll be re-potted.
You'll think - where did that come from?
It sounds so fresh and new!
But someone else inspired it -
it could even be you!
So never trust a poet
they are at least two-faced
though their work is eco friendly
as no word goes to waste.

Martin Grey

MUSEUM

Bulging bags in dingy basements
unsafely stow exhibits I collected
from our best abiding attempts at glories,
carefully numbered, catalogued,
cross-referenced with our future plans
and traded little stories.

I'd miss trying not to miss you,

but in my my bright rooms of empty displays
I build your legacies on sorrow;
while my ever-silent audio guides
talk in depth about the yesterdays
you find a way to weave
in my tomorrow.

I'd miss trying not to miss you,

but I curate my ripped-up info cards
in a cordoned off exhibit hall
of artefacts reimagined from within,
slowly losing you in me,
until I admit the entropy
of our eternal spin.

I'd miss trying not to miss you.

Richard Hawtree

WHILE READING LADY MONTAGU

'I loath the lewd rake, the dress'd fopling despise:
Before such pursuers the nice virgin flies:
And as OVID has sweetly in parables told,
We harden like trees, and like rivers grow cold.'
from 'The Lover: A Ballad' by Lady Mary Wortley Montagu (1689–1762)

While reading Lady Montagu
the panther in her heart
escapes from Rilke's poem
to outwit Augustan art.

While reading Lady Montagu
her atoms and her bees
collide in hailstorms racing
from the western Pyrenees.

While reading Lady Montagu
I'm rarely keen to please
as her women dance with Ovid
through their metamorphoses.

While reading Lady Montagu
I don't lose any time
collecting fresh hypocrisies
to skewer with my rhyme.

Karen Izod

VIGIL
Lighting a candle for Sarah Everard 13.3.21

I did once get pressed up against the wall
outside my office and not know how to
say, since he was himself, my boss.

And I did once see a man expose himself.
I thought it was only to me, in that country lane,
but time tells me these things are plural.

And years before, I did once cower under that bench
in the hope that they would give up their search
and I wouldn't need to think through the next step,
the hardened points of my ballet shoes my only weapon.

So I did light my candle,
though really would have preferred to swim
in that torrent of women, just being women
out for a night on the town.

Pete Jardine

SECRET BATH SPANIEL

I step out of the bath while the water drains
And conclude my ablutions
Glancing back to the tub before leaving the room
I am at once appalled and amazed.

It appears that whilst I was having my bath
Someone was also bathing a short haired spaniel
Who was clearly undergoing his spring moult
Leaving behind far, FAR too much evidence.

As I stare in silence at the sheer quantity of lost locks
Barbers Adagio for Strings begins to play
And memories of life with luxurious hair
Flood back all at once to pass before my eyes.

Looking out to sea, with the wind in my hair.
Riding my bicycle, with the wind in my hair.
Walking, …with hair.
Just, having hair.

I think I'd better stop using shampoo,
Start using adhesive.

Christopher Johnson

CAME BACK

From towns gone by now, folk waved as the fame,
Had passed up the tracks, ahead of the train,
Slowing…as kids run, short shouting out names,
A coming ne'er seen, heard or told again.

Some watchers just watch, not starting more verbs,
A breezed flyer flew the dream of a bird,
Come sun's rays split cloud to reign on the scene…
'…Slow kid, I'll whisper my place in this scheme.

Spread sand I'll magic to shuffling pulsed thing,
On tall stairs I'll float to the top tapping,
Twirled and so swirled to a tight coiling curl,
Then leap so high as…reach Neverland world.

See, I'm the Jangles, Billy Bo Jangles,
Through long times, for you, I've come back to…dance.'

Alex Josephy

FOR A JOURNEY TO THE FOREST IN TIME OF SNOW

Purse, dirk, night-cap, kerchief, shoeing-horn, buget, and shoes;
Spear, nails, hood, halter, sadle-cloth, spurs, hat, withy horse-comb;
Bow, arrow, sword, buckler, horn, brush, gloves, string, and thy
bracer…

from 'Memorial Verses for Travellers', Sir Anthony Fitzherbert

Three-layer face mask in a plastic zip-up freezer bag;
sapphire-blue sanitiser gel in handy-size bottle;
impregnated wipes, gloves, windscreen wiping rag;

iPhone, latest generation satnav app
with speed limit camera detection gizmo; flask
of fresh black coffee; recycled telescopic plastic cup;

for waiting at the lights, Leonard Cohen;
for the Eastway, Antonio Vivaldi;
for my forgetful soul: Find my Friend, Find my Phone;

passcode for the car park, code for woodpecker chat;
Fairisle hat with earflaps; badger-spotting glasses;
rolled and buckled picnic blanket for a little frozen nap;

miniature whisky for a hilltop glow;
bush-brown jacket, fur-lined boots, pack of Kleenex
for behind-hedge peeing; online guide to cloven tracks in snow.

Liz Lennie

ABED WITH THREE GREAT POETS OF THE TWENTIETH CENTURY
or the dangers of literature

So here lie I, like Hemingway, in bed with words again
(Though far from him in spirits, sex, sea and The War in Spain.)
Me, reading and writing on this and that
To escape from physical pain.

Yes, Will, Ez and Tom, my three poetic greats,
Mr. Eliot, Mr. Pound and Mr. Yeats,
Welcome to my wee world of Woking
From your Ireland, England and United States.

Though I have never held you close to me in bed
Your poetry resounds in the caverns of my head!
Your images flood my inward eye, I drown -
And sinking, can't forget a single word you said!

My first anthology, at school, Level O, was 'Reason and Rhyme'.
I had it all by heart, but did not know at that time
'The Fiddler of Dooney (Yeats) forever
In my inward ear would dance and chime.

Then off to Uni, I found other lilting loves besides Old Billyum
With his Isle of Innisfree, nine rows of beans and long road to
Byzantium.
I discovered America - Walt, Ezra and
That Anglo fellow, Old Possum.

His 'The Waste Land' o'erwhelmed me, a transatlantic depression.
'I grow old, I grow old, I shall wear ...' a different mask each session.
But now, my fellow writers, may I
Make my last confession?

I am an addict, a lost soul. I need a cure for my obsession,
To get myself off this hook,
To find my own feet, to rise above the book, the book ...
I should shut them all up, stand up,
Step out into another world.
Open to my own fresh look.

Andy B.J. Low

BIRTH OF A POET

There's a fight! There's a fight! Quick, come with me.
Gather 'round, block the view, so the teachers can't see.
There's a big gang of poets come to see who's the best
calling all-comers for a poetry contest.

Now, I'm curious and wary: A poetry contest?
That's an English exam. Those I detest.
Nine failed O-levels and one CSE.
Failed that as well, consistent is me.

I'd better revise and do some research.

So I went out and bought some of them poetry mags
got a feel for the stuff that's writ by these hacks.
The first thing I notice, and the next and the next,
is: It's bollocks, nothing rhymes and it's dreary as heck.

The stuff that I write is nothing like this.
I try to be open, but really, it's shit.
Obscure's the new clever, it's obtuse and unverse,
Some new form of art with its head up its arse.
and for line after line, while it's clearly not prose,
it's a catalogue of counterfeit Emperor's new clothes.

Then my musings are halted by a cacophonous roar
and I realise just how far is the stage from the door.
The bully calls out "We've not seen you before"
Makes a grab for my balls, but falls, face first to the floor.
(It's a neat little trick I may've practised before.)

Then thrust from the throng further into the ring
my pen dripping blood and ready to sting
In the silence that follows I know I will win
I look straight in his eye.

I begin.

Konstandinos Mahoney

MOVING ON

Last stroll down to the waterfront.
The port, dulled by familiarity,
is bright and strange again,
a ferry flickers in sea's diamond dazzle.
Moored to the quayside, sleek yachts,
a refugee dhow, a wide eye painted on its prow.
Restless, the world is restless.

Boot loaded, key turned, car trembles.
When you pack your bones and go
what music plays you out? -
the scrape of cicadas,
clatter of dice on a backgammon board,
shouts of children playing ball,
love song on the radio.

Alwyn Marriage

SPECULATE
post-covid

Is that woman in the mirror really me?
I touch the cold hard surface with my hand,
watch fingertips reflecting fingers meeting mine
as the light of truth betrays my fantasies, and
presents an image that I didn't want to see.

I know that my reflection in the glass
is an honest record of how I generally appear:
white hair, pale skin, no longer in my prime;
though how youth disappeared so quickly isn't clear,
it's obvious that all I loved and valued had to pass.

....

It's obvious that all I loved and valued had to pass,
though how youth disappeared so quickly isn't clear.
White hair, pale skin, no longer in my prime –
is an honest record of how I generally appear.

I know that my reflection in the glass
presents an image that I didn't want to see.
As the light of truth betrays my fantasies, and
I watch fingertips reflecting fingers meeting mine.
I touch the cold hard surface with my hand.
Is that woman in the mirror really me?

Tom McColl

THE CHALK FAIRY

Each night I traipse
the streets of London,
drawing chalk lines
round homeless people
sleeping rough.

I've found
that, even in the early hours
of Christmas Day,
there's no shortage of bodies
to draw my outlines round:
London's one big crime scene
every single day of the year.

Elaine McGinty

WILD FIRES

When rage sets the land alight
Innocent souls frozen in fright
Those with wings can take their flight
But others, burn who stay
And fight

Someone is picking up pieces
In silence and alone
The desolation is always borne
By the maker of the home

All of the golden eagles
Who apparently have all the vision
But no ability to see through
Ideological division

Ultimately it transpires
That manifests itself
As rage in the heart and wild fires
From unequal wealth

And yet we need
To see fire kill and heat our skin
For common bleed
Is not enough
For redemption to sink in

Anna Molesworth

PSEUDONARCISSUS

Do not offer me a pink daffodil.
Pink is not what daffodils are meant to be.
Pink is for cherry blossom, peonies, and roses,
Strawberry milkshake and baby-sick.
I do not want a pink daffodil.
I want the yellow essence of daffodil,
The grapefruit morning zing of daffodil,
The battery acid shock of daffodil,
the chilly handed slap of daffodil,
the icy water dawn plunge into daffodil
that wakes you from your winter numbness
to speak the truth of daffodil
and shouts:
'Awake! Awake! Awake!'

Heather Moulson

SLUMMY MUMMY

Slummy mummy, you keep me awake at night.
Standing there on your sticky kitchen floor,
with your unmade up face and strategically torn jeans.
Your voice hoarse from rowdy mealtimes,
finding pasta sauce and quinoa at the last minute.

Gazing out at the world through grimy windows,
over a butler sink full of unholy chaos.
Why don't you pour away that stagnant milk?
Or tidy the toys from your stairs before
Health & Safety break the door down?!

You pick up school uniform off the
loose boarded floor for the next day.
You are a walking disaster, so why do other
mothers fall over you at the school gates?
Anxious to bask in your seedy glamour,
while I steal off to iron sheets for children,
who only yearn to live with you.

Suzie Millar

FINAL ATTEMPT

I knock on the door.
Silence.
There is no keen response, just
a slab of painted yellow
staring at my face.

I knock again.
Silence.
Frustration bubbles up,
hurt that you won't answer,
here, or on the phone.

I knock again,
firmer blows,
determined you will hear but
thuds sink into silence,
I stand here feeling shamed.

To the side of the door a wooden bench
offers a place to sit. I settle myself, feel the sun
explore me as it yawns; soon it will be asleep.
I wake to find night has come,
the sky a fathomless space.

I knock on the door softly,
mindful of sleeping neighbours
innocent of our debate,
how words grew jagged edges,
pierced each other with hate.

Like an over-sized bouncer
protecting his club
the door refuses to budge.

My welcome here is done.

Su Mitchell

THREE LITTLE RATS

Three little rats came out to play
Over my bed not far away
Wrestled my fingers without fear
Sat on my head to inspect my ear

Three little rats came out to play
Over my bed not far away
One bit a hole in the end of the sheet
Two ran off to lick at my feet

Three little rats came out to play
Over my bed not far away
Ran round the room and had a ball
Stripped the paper from the wall

Three little rats came out to play
Over my bed not far away
Ate the toes of a pair of socks
Made a nest from my summer frock

Three little rats came out to play
Over my bed not far away
Found a corner of carpet to chew
Went to sleep in my husbands' shoe

Patrick Osada

REFUGEES

Escaping gunfire from the sea,
fear and blind panic drove them on
like any other refugees.
Without the lodestar of their lives –
away from the familiar –
they travelled unseen through the night
from far beyond the ocean's swell.

Singing, they kept their spirits high,
they passed Black Rock and Castle Point
to swing into the broad Porthcuel…
Beyond moored boats with jangling sheets,
the sleeping Manor House at Place,
they lost their way and chose Porth Creek.

Into this elemental place
of mudflats, long abandoned boats,
they moved in on a changing tide.
Beneath the overhanging oaks
where brown stream narrows, up near Froe,
the tidal waters ebbed away.

Caught up in flotsam, debris, weed,
the party floundered in the creek
as channel water turned to shoals.
Poor gardeners raised the alarm –
as sun rose on the carnage there,
of those who travelled from the sea,
only a handful still survived.

Now mouths are stopped – their chant has gone
and eyes are blind to helping hands
as men humped bodies to the grass.
There's tragedy, no respite won,
no refuge in this hostile land –
for those who've journeyed from so far
the sole lament is curlews' song.

Footnote: a large pod of dolphins was discovered beached in the shallows of Porth Creek, Cornwall – 26 had died.

Matthew Paul

SWIMMINGLY

wasn't how I swam. The tannoy enjoined, 'Will all
patrons wearing navy wristbands please leave the pool?'
Sunday mornings: Dad reminding Andrew and me
that public baths had been closed as contingency
during the war, for fear of what a direct hit
would do. Back home, the high-summer sky lit
its fuse—the liquorice-allsort blue of a jay—
over turquoised coppers in a Wedgwood ashtray.

To help bolster British car production, Dad blew
a wodge on a brand-new Metro, metallic-blue.
Dodging 'snarl-ups' on major roads and motorways,
he followed snaky dirt tracks and unmade byways.
Thus we proceeded on our annual holiday—
where I elbowed my crawl across the azure bay.

Geoffrey Pimlott

RUN SOFTLY

Run softly River Wandle
Down to Carshalton Chalkstream
Into Croydon
Out of Wandle Park
I stood on its bank
Watching it trickle past people's
Back gardens,
Then running under ground
Through tunnels
Beneath suburbs
Thornton Heath
Mitcham Marshes
Morden Merton
Past Earlsfield villages
Twisting down to Battersea
to join the Thames;
Prothalamion
Where wise poet
Edmund Spenser pondered
River, run softly
'Till I end my song
One stormy afternoon
A boy slipped in to fight its flood
Through Thor's thunderous cruelty
To quake and fear with such wild alarms
But Spenser's Muse
Rescued him
To run softly river Wandle
Make this stream
No child might suffer
In its flood to dwell
Bathe in Thames water
With the River Wandle
Down to Ocean's
For Edmund Spenser's poem written
On walls
Under river walk-ways arches
Blackfriars to London Bridge
Run down, 'Till this poet might end his song

Lorri Pimlott

THE SMALLEST HE OR SHE THAT IS IN ENGLAND

Somebody has to fell the trees
drain the marshes shape the land
move the stones dig the postholes
raise the stones drive the cattle
somebody has to be the sacrifice

Someone has to grind the grain
between the quern stones
bake the bread cook the meat
spin the wool weave the cloth
bear the baby rock the cradle

Someone had to wield the sabre
scythe the stalks ride the horse
thresh the grain at Peterloo
that someone might be
somebody's else's brother

Somebody has to throw the brick
shatter the glass lead the charge
rock the city harvest the rage
somebody has to shape the land
somebody has to be the sacrifice

Ray Pool

BYE BYE BLACKBIRD

Something about that eye
not seeing,
not knowing me there
is like a dream

of soaring free
the gripping of a branch
consensual sex on the wing.

Beside me now on the spade
while clawing at nothing,
it seems unconcerned

while the bright beads of bluebottles
steer her to the earth.

Chris Ross

SHOES

Gotta buy my gal a pair of Germaine Greer shoes
Shoes that lesser mortals would be afraid to Jimmy Choos
Shoes you can`t buy in Freeman Hardy and Who?
Not so much look at me more who the hell are you?
The sort of shoes that say I patently don`t care
The sort of killer heels that you could never wear
The sort of shoes that never need to say excuse me
They introduce themselves with dramatic mystery
Worn by the girl who knows she`s on top
You`ll never find a pair in a charity shop
London loafer leather with blue suede attitude
A little ego edgy they`re the right kind of rude
A short black leather jacket with faux fur trim
Discreetly knuckle dusted with just the right amount of bling
Nothing ostentatious maybe a hint of leopard print
You always turn heads You`ve got serious style
You walk the walk
You talk the talk
You`re way out in front by a moon walk mile
We make our way to the Brighton North Lanes
There`s a shoe shop there where no one ever complains
Why would they?
Devil may care footwear for fashionable feet
Platform soul food for the groovy elite
They cost a bloody fortune but no need for
Crocodile tears or blubbery boo-hoos
Who cares who wears the trousers
Only you can wear the shoes

Maggie Sawkins

SNAKE

He had it done on a whim
he told us, just before his spell
in Doolally.

Home from the war,
he lived with the regret –
no matter that we loved it.

Days at the beach he'd sit
with his shirt on, or lie forever,
his back to the sand.

It was a work of art
that began at his waist
and wound its way up

around the trunk
of a palm tree and ended
where we could see

its blue arrow tongue
flickering at the nape
of neck.

Carla Scarano

IN PRAISE OF RICE
To my husband

You stir the carnaroli rice in the pot with a wooden spoon.
The rice is overcooked, it thickens
in the receding boiling water.

You remove it from the hob and keep stirring
until the grains look fat enough,
ripe and glued one to the other.

You scoop small portions in bowls for me and our daughter,
then eat it straight from the pot
adding in plenty of olive oil and parmigiano,

mixing, savouring,
heaven in your eyes

Brit Shneuer

THE RESERVATION

A walk I will not take
in the Reservation when the night thick black curtain drops down
and for once a day, become unreserved

The invisible Nature Spirits
rolling in purple thorns, erase the walking path
for snakes and gazelles to pass,
bringing back the fireflies
Families of boars come out of their hiding bush to graze
on freshly dug roots and sweet Cactus fruits
Silver rippling of the mongoose backs glitter-vanish-glitter play in the
coloured black air
Foxes invite their mates,
to eat wild grapes, dig and burry and tussle in the sand
Howling jackals igniting each other to an orchestra of complaints
Leaves sipping dew crystals between the day's dusty grains
Goats hairy milky smell, linger among trees just received a goat's
haircuts
On rocks and boulders still sunny hot, geckoes sprawl

Do spiders sleep?

Trees communicating wordlessly, Innocent vulnerable filigrees

Who will praise the essences of milk, honey and olive oil?

Granting an amnesty to us all

My night is thick with inherited un-humanness

Afraid of the suffering this world can inflict

Retreat as the living entity of the trees

Nevertheless come round to germinate.

Peter Taylor

TWO LEAVES

We will bud green together,
a fresh, bright green,
and we will be washed together
by the same water cleaned.

We will be fed together
by the same moist earth and light
and a deeper green we'll turn together
as the days deny the nights.

Yes we will turn our backs together
when the South-west wind blows strong
and we will dance entwined together
as it softens into song.

And we will hide the sun together,
grant travellers cool shade;
and we will help them rest together
with every journey made.

It may be we will fall together
if lightning sears the branch,
the branch which we adorn together
will keep us close perchance.

And should we see greens turn together
to reds and browns and golds,
we'll play our glory days together
then watch ourselves grow old.

But we can't choose to fall together
if we reach deep autumn's end;
you may take your leave on a different breeze
and leave your love, your friend.

So let us watch and wait together,
until the wind blows true,
then, letting go our grip together,
I'll fly away with you.

Nick Toczek

THEM

Voted in by all us fools,
Millionaires make the rules,
Milk the system. They've the tools.

They laze by their heated pools,
Raise the price of foods and fuels,
Run the rackets. We're their mules.

Waiting while their champagne cools,
They close hospitals and schools.
Deaths don't phase them. They're like ghouls.

Butlers, ballrooms, vestibules,
Ancestors who died in duels,
They've kitchen staff. We've thin gruels.

In their world we're molecules,
There to swill their piss and stools.
We're worn out, while they wear jewels.

Anne Warrington

GEYSER BILL

We called him the old geyser,
The man who came to our church.
He took his job very seriously, did that old geyser:
Church wardening, maintenance, roof repairs,
        painting, heating, lighting candles
You name it, and he was onto it.

That old geyser at our church
Didn't care for kids, didn't care for people,
Didn't care to smile, didn't care to speak
But sang hymns loudly,
Gave loud responses, boring readings,
Suffered bouts of anger
For no real rhyme nor reason.

Churchgoers steered clear of that old geyser
Didn't dare greet him, whisper, laugh
Lest he gave a withering glance.
Under our breath, we called him the Devil's Spy
Sent to seize us and send us to a hellish place to fry.

Then one Sunday that old geyser
Failed to appear at Church
Nor the next.
The heating failed, candles were not lit!
Where was he, that old geyser?

Later, the Vicar announced that Bill, for Bill was his name,
        had chosen not to live but to die.
Tormented by flashbacks of massacres on
Normandy Beaches, from which he'd escaped —
though he'd often wondered why, so the letter said.
His place, he felt, was with his pals, those men who'd died.

After that we stopped calling him that old geyser
Forever afterwards he became known as Geyser Bill.

Richard Williams

HOLIDAY IN A PORTSMOUTH GARDEN

I bought my dreams of the open trail
beyond the humdrum thrum of city traffic,
but how these tracks were calcified,
as criss-crossed skies of wing-tipped stars
were cleared by a future that few could see.

Our lives made rivers filled deep with silt,
mouths dry from the loss of expectation,
so fragile this man-made dissonance,
we can't see what we already have
for fear of what might be lost.

A blackbird sings two gardens away,
trills above near silenced streets.
Forty days straight I have heard his call
as batteries drain down on racing time,
all this energy spent chasing clouds.

Belted in tight on my rolling road
paying for a journey I couldn't afford.
Now harmonies soar over warming walls,
the lilting notes of spring forgot –
so much I knew but did not know.

My open trail a trial no more,
aeroplanes grounded I travel at home.
All the mountains I leave unclaimed,
all the seas that I'll not sail,
slipping away with this blackbird's song.

Rodney Wood

THE NIGHT I TOLD GENESIS TO FUCK OFF
27 May 1972, Farnborough Tech

Chubby set up a trestle table inside and said to me
Mike was a student here and I've seen the band
practising at the Farnham Maltings. They're on fire!
I nodded, took the tickets from my old school friend.
The Melody Maker shakes hands with you on that,
I said, *Pass my Dad's regards on to yours.* The stairs
behind him went to room 306 where I spent two years
one night a week, studying, and failing, English A level.
Then to the bar with Frances for two halves of mild
and ten Embassy. The equipment on stage gathered dust
the drums and guitars waited like groupies but the band
were elsewhere - high, smoking spliffs, drinking while me
and Frances sat cross-legged on parquet flooring talking
about how I never spoke to Chubby at school, why I kept
failing English. I knew Brave New World, Two Cheers
for Democracy and Anthony and Cleopatra backwards.
It wasn't that, said Frances, *it was the essay, your*
teacher said you wrote funny and not in a good way.
Just then a smell of musk arrived followed by Jasper
with his ginger hair, swearing as usual and scratching
his nose. Then Nick came, striking a pose, and saying
Genesis sound *like a river of silver that glows,* lastly
Jon, who really made an effort to be hip with long hair,
wooden beads, flowery shirt, flares and suede boots.
He was posh and lived in Farnham, the nicest town
in Surrey. We sit and talk till the support come on
to play their dreamy cross of Bach and Bee Gees.
An interval, time for two more glasses of mild then
ex-public schoolboys, Genesis, amble from the wings
and they looked earnest, the real deal for a few seconds
until the lead singer came on dressed as a daffodil
and sang, *Walking across the sitting-room / I turn the television off*
Sitting beside you, I look into your eyes / As the sound of motorcars
fades. Frances didn't like this bunch of posers. Jon and Nick
thought they were the best band ever. An hour later
Daffy shouted *Do you want more?* I yelled back *Fuck off.*
The hall was silent and the band slunk off stage.
My girlfriend gave me a kiss and that was the best
thing I've ever done.   Telling Genesis to fuck off.

Jacky Woods

BEGINNINGS

I touch surfaces of the house that was
my skin and bone for over sixty years,
I am a lover hungry to devour
the body I once took for granted,
needing to leave my imprint on her flesh.

I run my fingers along artexed walls,
dust encrusted within its ridges,
I clutch the banister in a last embrace,
climb the stairs for the final time,
arms heavy with dreams.

I trace the lines of Julia's wall painting,
the contours of Utopian bodies she had drawn
when we were sixteen.
I follow faded beams of light emanating
from the hand of an undisclosed deity.

In my mother's bedroom I place my ear next
to the wallpaper to hear the echo of my heartbeat.
Folding myself into the dressing gown
still hanging behind the door,
I breathe in the fibres of her sleep.

The flotsam of cobwebbed corners
sticks greyly to my clothes
as tenderly I explore the scars
left from pictures that once adorned
these walls but now are stacked away.
.
My fingertips skate across the gallery
of reflections in the hallway mirror
the refraction of changing images
from child, adolescent, middle aged woman,
to the rootless ghost I will become.

The door handle is cold to touch.
I think of all the strangers
who will enter,
sit down, begin again.

BIOGRAPHIES

David Andrew was born in Manchester in 1939. After retiring as a civil servant, he became editor of Write Out Loud's Gig Guide, and was a keen supporter of Write Out Loud Woking and open-mic poetry. He published two collections of poetry, and his poems appeared in numerous magazines. Much to his surprise he became a grandfather, very late in life, after he had turned 80. He died in 2022 at the age of 82.

Chris Andrews has had over 60 poems published in small press poetry magazines.

Aileen Ballantyne's poetry collection *Taking Flight* (Luath Press) includes a series of poems on the Lockerbie disaster, which won the prestigious Mslexia Poetry Prize (2015). Aileen was formerly staff Medical Correspondent for The Guardian, then The Sunday Times. Recordings of her poems are available at the Scottish Poetry Library website https://www.scottishpoetrylibrary.org.uk/poet/aileen-ballantyne/

Trevor Breedon started writing poetry in 2014 after a career as a sub-editor in newspaper journalism. He has been published in several anthologies but has yet to produce a pamphlet or collection. He lives near Canterbury, Kent

Trisha Broomfield lived in Australia as a child and now lives with her husband in Surrey. She writes poetry, short stories and unfinished crime novels. She has two pamphlets published by Dempsey and Windle, *When Peter Sellers Came to Tea* and *Husbands for Breakfast*, contributed to *Surrey Libraries Poetry Blog, Words in Focus, Places of Poetry, BBC Radio Surrey* and *Spilling Cocoa Over Martin Amis.*

Graham Brown was born in Aldershot in 1953. Has written poetry since 1976 and has appeared at many venues up and down the country. Ran 'Stand and Deliver' Open Mic in Newcastle Upon Tyne between 1996 and 2000. Now based on the Isle of Wight and running regular Open Mic events in Newport and Ryde. Quirky, jokey, poignant, thoughtful. Does more than it says on the tin. One half of the Unofficial Secrets Act.

Denise Bundred has an MA in Creative Writing and is a Fellow of the Royal College of Physicians. She won the Hippocrates Prize 2016, coming second in 2019. She has poems in various poetry anthologies and magazines. *Litany of a Cardiologist* was published by Against the Grain Press in 2020.

Lee Campbell is an artist, poet, filmmaker and Senior Lecturer at University of the Arts London. His poems have featured in *The Atticus Review, Ink, Sweat and Tears, Powders Press* and *Queerlings – A Literary Magazine for Queer Writing.* He tweets @leejjcampbell

Pratibha Castle's award-winning debut pamphlet *A Triptych of Birds and A Few Loose Feathers* (Hedgehog Poetry Press) was published

2022. Appearing widely in print and online including *Agenda, IS&T, London Grip* and *High Window,* she was highly commended and long-listed in competitions including Bridport Prize and Welsh Poetry Competition. A regular reader for The Poetry Place, West Wilts Radio, her second book is forthcoming this year.
www.pratibhacastlepoetry.com @pratibhacastle

Afon Claerwen flows through the mountains west of Rhayadar. In cold November 1966 it refreshed, guided and inspired an exhausted young soldier to complete one mission and start another, from warrior to poet. Not enough Welsh to be a bard, but another voice to inspire a kinder warrior for peace. Afon is also known as Dai Williams, blogs at www.afon.org

Stephen Claughton has published two pamphlets, *The War with Hannibal* (Poetry Salzburg, 2019) and *The 3-D Clock* (Dempsey & Windle, 2020). He reviews poetry for The High Window and London Grip and blogs occasionally at www.stephenclaughton.com, which has links to his poems and reviews.

Kitty Coles's poems have been widely published and have been nominated for the Forward Prize, Pushcart Prize and Best of the Net. Her pamphlet, *Seal Wife* (2017), was joint winner of the Indigo Dreams Pamphlet Prize. Her first collection, *Visiting Hours*, was published in 2020 by The High Window. For more information see www.kittyrcoles.com

Michael Cutchey wrote his first poem at 6 years old, but did not pursue the art form seriously until 2009, having written over eight hundred poems (and counting!) since. His work often deals with dark and sombre themes such as bereavement, depression, grief and mental illness. He considers his poetry an attempt to find catharsis in the gothic, the uncanny & the esoteric. He can often be seen wondering Guildford town centre in signature black clothing including hat & cane.

Dónall Dempsey is from the Curragh, Ireland. He has 5 poetry collections and has performed in the UK, Ireland, New Delhi and France. He has been translated into Irish, Italian, Spanish and Tamil. He delights in sound and the telling of stories and is honoured to have his words translated into other tongues. www.facebook.com DonallDonall, www.dempseyandwindle.com/donall-dempsey

Janice Dempsey is based in Guildford, began writing and performing poetry seriously after retiring from teaching art. Since 2016 she has been co-owner and editor, with her husband Dónall, of Dempsey & Windle, an independent poetry publishing company. Websites: janice-dempsey.com, dempseyandwindle.com, @DandWpublishing

John de Prey was raised on a remote farm bordering a wild private wood. With his five siblings he enjoyed trespassing, hiding from the owner behind trees; but John would later return alone. Thus a lifetime of travel was born. His poetry seemed naturally to grow from travel journal writing and he now finds it so exciting it's his form of bungee jumping. However "publishing" and competitions have never interested him. He writes for a great great grandchild who might find his poems and journals in an old trunk.

Alex de Suys, sometimes known as Baron Susius, but strangely not when he's making incendiary statements all over the Internet, is a satirist and social commentator with a penchant for rhyme. He can be seen at various open mics making people inhale sharply, although less and less these days. Now he sees a lot more nodding and even a little air punching. "They want 7.5 billion of us dead", he is often heard to quip amusingly. Fun times.

Shaun Fallows was born with Cerebral Palsy, but is a firm believer that his disability has given more than it has taken away, he has performed at open mic nights throughout the north west and, more recently, further afield appearing at Write Out Loud Woking via Zoom and Edinburgh BHP free fringe with his own show entitled Sunny And Chair He self-published his first book of poems entitled *Access-Ability* (2019) and in March of this year published his 2nd full collection entitled *They Race Me In The Streets* (2022) https://www.lulu.com/shop/shaun-fallows/ access-ability/paperback/product-24337793.html

Andy V. Frost is a lifelong Merton biker who when not finding an excuse to go for a ride has written and performed poetry for about twenty years. After motorcycles and wanderlust, he likes most arts, natural beauty and flying Kites.

Greg Freeman believes he has learned how to speak in public while co-compering Write Out Loud Woking. He is in danger of falling in love with the sound of his own voice.

Gillian Freeman has been a loyal supporter of Write Out Loud Woking since its first days at the New Inn, but has only lately been inspired to join in. Painting, rather than poetry, is her first love, but she is also extremely fond of one of the WOLW comperes.

Robert Garnham AKA Professor of Whimsy, was born in Woking. He's a spoken word artist performance and comedy poet who has performed all over the UK. For more information see https://professorofwhimsy.com

Sharron Green is a 'poet of a certain age' whose writing blends elements of nostalgia, comments on modern life and odes to nature. She enjoys experimenting with rhymes and poetic forms. Sharron has published *Introducing Rhymes n Roses* and *Viral Odes* and has contributed to over ten international anthologies. In 2021 she completed an MA in Creative Writing at the University of Surrey. Instagram, Facebook & Twitter: @rhymes_n_roses Website: https://rhymesnroses.com

Martin Grey is a Nottingham based poet, originally from Guildford, and co-director of World Jam. He mostly writes about connection, empathy, love, childhood and roundabouts. His first collection, *The Prettyboys of Gangster Town*, was published in 2020 by Fly on the Wall Poetry. www.martingreypoet.com

Richard Hawtree's poems have appeared in literary magazines including: *The Stinging Fly*, *The Honest Ulsterman*, *Banshee*, *Nine Muses Poetry* and *The Seventh Quarry*. New work is forthcoming in *The Stony Thursday Book* and *Black Bough Poetry*. His collection *The Night I Spoke Irish in Surrey* was published by Dempsey & Windle in 2019.

Karen Izod is an academic in the NHS, writer on wild places, thin places, city spaces, people, politics. Karen's poetry is published in a number of anthologies, on-line and in magazines, including *Agenda* and *Interpreter's House*. She is a 2021 winner of Coast to Coast to Coast's single poet competition. www.karenizod.com

Pete Jardine was born on Tyneside and moved south to escape the football mania. He started composing long narrative rhyming poems in his head while commuting and eventually performed a few of them at the Boiler Room and there he met the welcoming local poetry crowd. A natural born electronics design engineer, he has always been an imposter to the arts scene but found he enjoyed infiltrating the scene and lowering the bar for everybody. His output has consequently been very varied and extremely inconsistent.

Christopher Johnson is a writer based in West Sussex, to date, he has published four books of verse. With a fifth scheduled for release in late 2022. His work has also appeared in anthologies, magazines and regional press. He regularly performs at spoken word events in the West Midlands and Surrey. Interests and topics are diverse but a 'perennial philosophy' approach is a common factor. Sonnet structures are predominantly used as bases from which experimentation may flame. A practising Buddhist and advocate of 'true' value creation, Nam Myoho Renge Kyo.

Alex Josephy's 2020 collection, *Naked Since Faversham*, was published by Pindrop Press; her new pamphlet *Again Behold the Stars* is forthcoming from Cinnamon Press, spring 2023. Her poems have won the McLellan and Battered Moons prizes, and have appeared in magazines and anthologies in the UK, Italy and India. Website: www.alexjosephy.net

Liz Lennie has written creatively while growing up on a farm, at school and Art School near Guildford, then Newcastle University, V.S.O. In Singapore, teaching in Newcastle and Woking, mothering and organising farm visits. Relatively unpublished, she flourishes in Woking Writers Circle. She also loves art, photography and her garden.

Andy B J Low Having spectacularly failed English O-level nine times and GCSE English once Andy slunk off to become a research chemist, an electronic engineer then a computer programmer and finally an idiot, although some say this underlying trait was present throughout. It was during this last phase that he started to poet.

Konstandinos (Dino) Mahoney, based in London and the Greek island of Aegina, is of Greek-English-Irish heritage. He won publication of his second collection, *The Great Comet Of 1996 Foretells* in the Live Canon Poetry Collection Competition 2021. His first collection, *Tutti Frutti* was a sentinel publication poetry book competition winner. Dino is also a Poetry Society's Stanza Competition winner. He teaches Creative Writing at Hong Kong University (visiting lecturer), and is rep for Barnes and Chiswick Stanza. He is also part of *Dino and the Diamonds* a group that performs his poems as songs.

Alwyn Marriage's fifteen books include poetry, fiction and non-fiction and she's widely published in magazines, anthologies and on-line. Her latest books are *The Elder Race* (fiction), and *Pandora's Pandemic* and *Possibly a Pomegranate* (both poetry). For the last 14 years she's been Managing Editor of Oversteps Books. www.marriages.me.uk/alwyn

Tom McColl lives in London, and has had two poetry collections published: *Being With Me Will Help You Learn* (Listen Softly London Press, 2016) and *Grenade Genie* (Fly on the Wall Press, 2020). He's read at Write Out Loud Woking three times, including once as a feature, in September 2019.

Elaine McGinty Writer & singer now performing in a poetry & bass duo. Poetry has been published in *For The Many, Not The Few, Razur Cuts* & is part of *She Leads Change*. She has set up small festivals, co-founded non profit Phoenix Cultural Centre CIC/Fiery Bird Venue & presents Fiery Bird radio show.

Anna Molesworth was born in London in 1960 and studied art and drama at Trent Polytechnic (now University of Nottingham, Trent) as part of a Creative Arts degree. She has lived in Woking since 1989.

Suzie Millar believes poetry is a beautiful medium through which to explore life – both her own and that of others. Prompted by lockdown to creep out of her shell she now enjoys sharing her poems live and on paper.

Su Mitchell was born, and lived in Bradford since 1964. After 14 years, work related trauma triggered mental health issues and she started to write poetry as part of the healing process, daily life and the antics of her pet rats have been her source of inspiration over the years.

Heather Moulson has been writing and performing poetry since 2017. She has performed extensively around London, Guildford and of course, Woking. Her pamphlet *Bunty I Miss You* was published in 2019. Heather also loves to sketch, especially her black cat Dobby!

Patrick B. Osada recently retired as reviews editor for SOUTH poetry magazine. He has published seven collections, *From The Family Album* was launched in October 2020. Patrick's work has been broadcast on national and local radio and widely published in magazines, anthologies and on the internet. www.poetry-patrickosada.co.uk

Matthew Paul's collection, *The Evening Entertainment*, was published by Eyewear in 2017. His two collections of haiku – *The Regulars* and *The Lammas Lands* – and co-written/edited (with John Barlow) anthology, *Wing Beats: British Birds in Haiku*, were published by Snapshot Press. He lives in Rotherham, blogs at matthewpaulpoetry.blog and tweets @MatthewPaulPoet.

Geoffrey Pimlott's a painter who's been waxing lyrical in poetic form for 30 years. Encouraged to put pen to paper in a free-verse form in Surrey to those who will kindly listen!

Lorri Pimlott was born in England, but spent part of her childhood in NZ and Australia. Since then she has lived in several other countries, but is now settled near Guildford. Her poems often reflect her interest in history and the natural world, particularly the landscape and history of England.

Ray Pool is a pianist and amateur photographer who is intrigued by how images can inspire poetry, which he reads and writes avidly. His work, published in several anthologies and in pamphlets, offers views of the strange landscape of human behaviour against unlikely backdrops, with an emphasis on dark humour.

Chris Ross's poetry is mostly observational - standing on the sidelines and watching and listening. He performs as "chris the postman poet". He's also started posting videos on YouTube and he really is a postman.

Maggie Sawkins's new collection, *The House Where Courages Lives*, is published by Waterloo Press. Maggie lives in the Station Master's House at Brading Station on the Isle of Wight. Greg was a frequent visitor and supporter of Tongues and Grooves Poetry and Music Club which Maggie ran in Portsmouth for many years. http://www.hookedonwords.me/

Carla Scarano D'Antonio lives in Surrey with her family. She obtained her Master of Arts in Creative Writing at Lancaster University and has published her creative work in various magazines and reviews. Carla jointly won the first prize of the Dryden Translation Competition 2016 for translations of Eugenio Montale's poems. *Negotiating Caponata* was published in July 2020. She received a PhD in April 2021 for her work on Margaret Atwood at the University of Reading. She blogs at http://carlascarano.blogspot.com

Brit Shneuer lives in Israel, in a Haifa district town, is married and has a daughter and grandson. Worked as an actress in the repertory theatre, films and television in Israel for 10 years. Self published her first poetry book in December 2021 *The Cat Comes and with her the Garden.*

Peter Taylor started writing in 2012, quickly becoming bewitched by the idea that poetry was an infinite mode of expression and assimilation. In 2015 he won Paragram's chapbook prize and in 2016 was a finalist in the Poetry Rivals Slam competition. He has been published on numerous occasions in response to requests for submissions and spreads awareness of his work by running poetry afternoons in care homes, reading in hospices and embellishing complementary journals and websites with examples of his work.

Nick Toczek is a much-published writer and performer for adults and for children. He's from Bradford in Yorkshire. For more about him, please check out his website which is www.nicktoczek.com.

Anne Warrington One of the joys of retirement has been to rediscover her love of drama and reading and writing poetry. Since entering the third age she's been a drama judge for Arts Richmond, established Performance Poetry sessions at the Adelaide Pub in Twickenham and edited two Poetry Anthologies, namely *Through the Keyhole* and *Poems for Ukraine*. Profits from the latter going to British-Ukrainian Aid. Another joy has been to meet up with poets from other poetry groups, e.g. Write Out Loud, Woking thus dipping into the great wealth of poetry being written by people from all walks of life. It's been a privilege.

Richard Williams lives in Portsmouth, with his wife, diabetic cat and occasional returning children. He's had over 120 poems appear in various print and online magazines; others have been broadcast on the radio or turned into film. A first collection, *Landings*, was published by Dempsey & Windle in 2018.

Rodney Wood has been writing seriously for the past 20 years and enjoying the whole process. He's co-host of WOL and the Woking Stanza rep. WOL has taught him there are many styles and approaches of writing and performing which are all worthy of accolades. Best things about the monthly meetings – they're relaxed, open and great fun. He's published two pamphlets *Dante Called You Beatrice* and *When Listening Isn't Enough*.

Jacky Woods was born in Ipswich Suffolk, a place very dear to her heart. She has lived in the North West for many years. She enjoys reading at open mics both in person and on zoom. She has had several poems published in local and national publications and has published two of her own collections. She retired from teaching early because of ill health and is now a volunteer for the Reader charity.

Printed in Great Britain
by Amazon

86382823R00041